DEAR CATHOLIC FRIEND

Dear Catholic Friend:

Your letter is before me, and prayerfully I take time to answer it. The truth of God is so holy that I must deal very reverently with it. And the truth has been so perverted by Roman dogma and tradition, that the truth will not be palatable to you, I fear. Whether you will listen to it, whether your heart is open at all to the facts, I do not know. But in the blessed Word of God, I John 4:6 says: "We are of God: he that knoweth God heareth us; he that is not of God heareth not us. Hereby know we the spirit of truth, and the spirit of error." If in the heart you know Christ as Saviour, and if God's Spirit dwells in you, then God's Spirit will bear witness to you of the truth. And if there is no such witness, then I will conclude, of course, that you are in spiritual darkness. For we are told: "But the natural man receiveth not the things of the Spirit of God: for they are foolishness unto him: neither can he know them, because they are spiritually discerned" (I Cor. 2:14).

Note I do not say that if you do not agree with me in every detail, you are not saved, you are not a child of God. But I speak of the truth as it is in the Word of God, simple and plain, on major matters. If your heart is not open to principal truth from the Word of God, then the Spirit of God is not abiding in you and you will go on in your blindness. I will grieve about that if you do. But I hope that there is in you a love for Christ and the presence of the Holy Spirit of God so that your heart will answer honestly to the Scriptures. If it does not, then at least I have done my duty.

I. The Roman Church Has Brought Upon Itself the Curse of Revelation 22:18, 19, by Adding to the Scripture.

Unbelieving men sometimes take from the Word of God,

minimize parts of it, say it is not true and is not binding. The Roman Church and some others have the same kind of sin, in that they take the traditions of men, the decrees and doctrines of men, and add them to what the Bible says, thus often nullifying parts of the Bible. And to those who do so, God plainly says: "For I testify unto every man that heareth the words of the prophecy of this book, If any man shall add unto these things, God shall add unto him the plagues that are written in this book" (Rev. 22:18). The statement in the Bible is simple. Honest people can understand it. To try to evade the meaning of the Scripture will prove insincerity. To add obligations or authority or rules or doctrines to those in the Bible, and to bow to authority beside the authority of the Bible and the authorities plainly given in the Bible means to bring the curse, the plagues written in the book of Revelation, to those who add thus to the canon of Scripture their opinions and organizations and traditions and rules and doctrines.

Some bring God's curse on them by marking off part of the Bible, calling it erroneous, uninspired, less than the very Word of God. Others achieve the same effect by setting up another authority beside the Bible which steals from the Bible part of its own God-given authority. So Mormons have the Book of Mormon and add it to God's Word. So Christian Scientists have the writings of Mrs. Mary Baker Eddy and add them to the authority of the Bible. So Seventh-Day Adventists have often, in the past, added the writings of Mrs. White and called them authoritative and inspired like the Bible. And so the Roman Catholic organization puts up the authority of a church, the traditions of church, the rulings of popes and councils, and thus would drain away the real authority that God has put in the Word of God. And so Roman Catholicism takes its place as a false cult and must be so recognized by those who accept the authority of the Bible itself, the authority which it claims beyond any possible doubt, the authority which Christ Himself recognized in the Bible.

Jesus quoted to the Pharisees the words of Isaiah about people who honor God with their lips but whose heart is far from Him.

> "He answered and said unto them, Well hath Esaias prophesied of you hypocrites, as it is written, This people honoureth me with their lips, but their heart is far from me. Howbeit in vain do they worship me, teaching for doctrines the commandments of men. For laying aside the commandment of God, ye hold the tradition of men, as the washing of pots and cups: and many other such like things ye do. And he said unto them, Full well ye reject the commandment of God, that ye may keep your own tradition."–Mark. 7:6–9.

Pharisees were hypocrites because they gave only nominal and verbal assent to the Scriptures and really they worshiped God in vain, "teaching for doctrines the commandments of men." And Jesus accused them, "Full well ye reject the commandment of God, that ye may keep your own tradition." Honest people could not say that the Pharisees did not add to the commands of God with their tradition and commandments of men. And every student in the matter must know, and you are intelligent enough to know, that the Roman Church has added to the commandments of God even more than did the Pharisees in Bible times. They make traditions of men take the place of the commandments of God. You pretend to be for the Bible, to accept its authority. You even claim that you accept the authority of the church *on the authority of the Bible.* Then you must accept what Jesus said on the matter or accept His brand as a hypocrite on certain matters.

1. The Bible plainly forbids making any image for worship and bowing down to any image.

> "Thou shalt not make unto thee any graven image, or any likeness of any thing that is in heaven above, or that is in the earth beneath, or that is in the water under the earth. Thou shalt not bow down thyself to them, nor serve them: for I the LORD thy God am a jealous God, visiting the iniquity of the fathers upon the children unto the third and fourth generation of them that hate me."–Exod. 29:4, 5.

And any honest reader knows that that Scripture forbids using an image in worship, bowing down to it, praying before it, and serving it. And yet the Catholic Church not only has images, but encourages people to pray to images, to the crucifix, to images of Mary, to images of saints. Here Roman tradition violates the Bible, and the commandments of men take the place of the commandments of God. That is sin.

2. The Scriptures command that "a bishop then must be blameless, the husband of one wife..." (I Tim. 3:2).

The Roman Church says that a bishop must have no wife at all. It even makes foolish pretensions that Peter put away his wife, though there is not a scratch of history in the Bible or out to indicate anything of the kind. It is a clear case of putting human tradition ahead of the Bible.

3. Jesus Christ plainly taught that Mary was on the same plane with all other Christians who would do the will of God.

> *"There came then his brethren and his mother, and, standing without, sent unto him, calling him. And the multitude sat about him, and they said unto him, Behold, thy mother and thy brethren without seek for thee. And he answered them, saying, Who is my mother, or my brethren? And he looked round about on them which sat about him, and said, Behold my mother and my brethren! For whoso-ever shall do the will of God, the same is my brother, and my sister, and mother."*–Mark. 5:31–35.

Do not avoid the truth here on the authority of Jesus Christ, "Whosoever shall do the will of God, the same is my brother, and my sister, and mother." And when one heard Jesus and cried out, "Blessed is the womb that bare thee, and the paps which thou hast sucked," Jesus answered, "Yea rather, blessed are they that hear the word of God, and keep it" (Luke 11:27,28). There is no hint in the Bible that New Testament Christians ever regarded Mary as more than another good woman. She had no authority among the apostles. No one was taught to pray to her, to do her homage, to adore her, or to partake of the unscriptural worship which Catholics do, but call it by other names. Thus the Roman Church has brought a plague upon itself by adding the commandments of men and traditions of men to the commands of God.

4. The Roman Catholic mass disregards the Word of God to add sacrifices for sin contrary to the explicit Word of God.

In Hebrews 10:8-14 is a very clear pronouncement from God that when Christ died on the cross, that did away with all other sacrifices. It reads:

> "Above when he said, Sacrifice and offering and burnt-offerings and offering for sin thou wouldest not, neither hadst pleasure therein; which are offered by the law; Then said he, Lo, I come to do thy will, O God. He taketh away the first, that he may establish the second. By the which will we are sanctified through the offering of the body of Jesus Christ once for all. And every priest standeth daily ministering and offering oftentimes the same sacrifices, which can never take away sins: But this man, after he had offered one sacrifice for sins for ever, sat down on the right hand of God; From henceforth expecting till his enemies be made his footstool. For by one offering he hath perfected for ever them that are sanctified."

This Scripture explicitly says certain things. It says (a) "Sacrifice and offering and burnt-offerings and offering for sin thou wouldest not, neither hadst pleasure therein; which are offered by the law." (b) He expressly says that He did away with the old sacrifices to establish a second. (c) And then He expressly says that the offering of Jesus Christ "once for all" settles the whole matter of sin. Again, He says, "But this man, after he had offered one sacrifice for sins for ever, sat down on the right hand of God." When Jesus had paid for all sins and offered the last sacrifice which settled things forever, then He sat down because His sacrificial work was done. (d) There is no need for further sacrifice, "for by one offering he hath perfected for ever them that are sanctified," that is, them that are set apart for God by the blood of Christ.

Then in the following verses the Lord reminds us of the promise in the Old Testament that He would make a new covenant with men, that He would put the law in their hearts and minds, and He says: "And their sins and iniquities will I remember no more. Now where remission of these is, there is no more offering for sin" (Heb. 10:17, 18).

Now notice the one grand summing-up statement: "Now

where remission of these is, there is no more offering for sin." When one has trusted Christ and had his sins forgiven, then "there is no more offering for sin," no more animal sacrifices, no more of any other kind of sacrifices.

So to make the mass a sacrifice, to claim that in the mass Jesus is sacrificed again and again, that the bread becomes His body, that the wine becomes His blood, and that there is saving virtue in this sacrifice–that is a blasphemous rejection of the Bible in favor of traditions of men. That is a false religion, not the Christian religion. Thus Roman Catholic friends, however good their intentions, have made in vain the commandments of God by their traditions.

There is not a single hint anywhere in the entire New Testament that New Testament Christians had any kind of sacrifices. The Lord's Supper was a memorial supper, a simple object lesson, a spiritual reminder that Christ had died for us and we are saved by His blood, and a simple and sweet reminder to all Christians that we belong to God and ought to love Him and serve Him and enter into His death. There is not a single hint in the entire Bible that there was any saving virtue in the communion. There is no hint that anybody ever was invited to take the communion or the Lord's Supper in Bible times except as he had already found peace with God and was already forgiven and saved.

5. The Roman Catholic Church has perverted the Bible and substituted tradition in making priests out of preachers or elders.

Since the Bible clearly teaches that now there is to be no more sacrifice for sins, and since the Old Testament priesthood has been succeeded by one priest, Jesus Christ, who has offered one sacrifice for-ever, then there is no teaching of a priesthood to offer sacrifices in the New Testament. There are elders, preachers. Some of these elders had official positions as pastors or supervisors of local congregations. It is true that in the spiritual sense, all Christians are to be "kings and priests unto God" (I Pet. 2:9; Rev. 5:10). But there was no official priestly work done by anyone as an officer of a church, as an elder or bishop in Bible times. It was not even specified that an elder or bishop should even be present when people took the Lord's Supper. It had no official significance. It was a simple, little object lesson, a ceremony of remembrance. And there is not a single hint anywhere that the Lord's Supper had any saving power. It was not a sacrifice. It was never called that in the Bible. That is a false doctrine, manufactured by the Church of Rome, which contradicts the Bible, adds to the Bible, and so brings the plagues of the Bible upon the Roman Church.

I have not room here to discuss all the innovations, all the strange and unscriptural doctrines and practices which have been invented by Roman Catholic hierarchy. In the Bible there was no pope and no papal authority, no papal infallibility. There were no prayers to Mary, no doctrine of Mary's Immaculate Conception nor of her body's ascension to Heaven. There were no penances, no indulgences, no confessions to priests, no orders of monks or nuns. All of this is manufactured, not only without the Bible but contrary to the plain teachings of the Word of God.

II. The Roman Catholic Idea of a Church Is Wholly Unknown in the Bible and Contrary to the Bible.

You tell me, dear friend, that the Catholic Church is "the true church." But you found no such term in the Bible and no such idea in the Bible. The Bible says nothing about any nationwide or world-wide organization. The idea of a church as a denomination is utterly foreign to the Bible. No such organization can be "the true church" because nothing like that is pictured or promised in the Bible. They had nothing like that in Bible times.

1. Churches in the New Testament were local congregations of believers.

The Bible speaks often in such language as "the church of God which is at Corinth" (I Cor. 1:2). "The church which was at Jerusalem" (Acts 8:1). But do not think that this was simply a segment of the general church. No, for the Scripture much more often uses the plural form for churches like "then had the churches rest throughout all Judea and Galilee and Samaria..." (Acts 9:31). Every congregation was a separate church, not part of a general church. "The churches of Galatia" (I Cor 16:1). "The churches of Asia" (I Cor. 16:19). "The churches of Macedonia" (II Cor. 8:1). "The churches of Galatia" (Gal. 1:2). "The seven churches which are in Asia" (Rev. 1:4).

We see then that in Bible practice and Bible terminology every local congregation was a separate church. If there were more than one, they were still "churches," plural; not "a church" or "the church."

And thus all the officers of New Testament times, the elders or pastors or bishops and the deacons, were officers of local congregations. There were no bishops over a certain territory or province, nor over a number of churches. That whole idea invented by Roman Catholicism is patterned after this world and is not only not found in the Bible but is contrary to the explicit teachings of the Bible. And many denominations have followed Rome in this false practice of area-wide denominations or "churches" which are not churches in the Bible sense.

2. The general term "church" is occasionally used referring to the whole body of Christ, all the saved, without any reference to any organization.

The word *church* in the New Testament is translated from the Greek word *ecclesia* and it always means a called-out assembly. That Greek word is translated everywhere in the New Testament as "church," except in three cases in Acts 19 where in verses 32, 39, and 41 it is translated "assembly," referring to the mob called out at Ephesus. More than ninety times the word *church* or *churches* is used about local congregations. A few times, eight or ten times, it is used in the larger sense of the whole body of Christ. In every such case it refers to that "general assembly and church of the firstborn, which are written in heaven" (Heb. 12:22, 23), those who will be called out at the rapture when Jesus comes, and then it will be literally a called-out assembly. It is in that sense that "Christ also loved the church, and gave himself for it" in Ephesians 5:25. It refers to every person born again and saved by the blood of Christ. The Lord Jesus never hinted that He was giving Himself for any organization, any so-called "true church" or denomination. For the Church of Rome to claim that it is this one body for whom Christ died is blasphemous, a perversion of the Scripture with an idea wholly unknown in the Bible.

3. The foolish idea that the church is founded on Peter is contrary to Scripture and historically false.

The Scripture says as plainly as it can be said that Jesus Christ is the foundation on which Christians are built, and that there is no other foundation. In I Corinthians 3:10,11, Paul was inspired to write:

> *"According to the grace of God which is given unto me, as a wise masterbuilder, I have laid the foundation, and another buildeth thereon. But let every man take heed how he buildeth thereupon. For other foundation can no man lay than that is laid, which is Jesus Christ."*

Paul as a wise masterbuilder laid the foundation. That is, he got people saved. He got them to trust in Christ. They are built on Christ. And then he plainly said, "For other foundation can no man lay than that is laid, which is Jesus Christ." And it is wise to go back and see the context in the same chapter. There was a division in Corinth over this very matter. He says in verse 4, "For while one saith, I am of Paul; and another, I am of Apollos; are ye not carnal?" And then he closes the chapter by saying: "Therefore let no man glory in men. For all things are your's; Whether Paul, or Apollos, or Cephas, or the world, or life, or death, or things present, or things to come; all are your's; And ye are Christ's; and Christ is God's" (vss. 21–23).

"Cephas" here is Peter. So here divine inspiration in the Bible plainly says that the church and salvation are not built on Paul or Apollos or on Cephas, and that men are not to glory in men, that is, none of these three men nor any others.

So Peter is not the foundation on which Christians are built.

He is not the foundation of the church. Christ is the foundation of the church.

But you say, as Catholic dogma teaches you to say and not from any independent study of the Scriptures, which you are not allowed to do—you say that Christ said He would build a church on Peter. You refer to Matthew 16:18, which the Catholic dogma currently teaches (but did not always so teach), that Christ founded the church on Peter. But read it: "And I say also unto thee, That thou art Peter, and upon this rock I will build my church; and the gates of hell shall not prevail against it." Now does Jesus here contradict the other Scriptures and say that the church is founded on Peter instead of on Himself? No indeed. Here there is a Greek play upon the words, "Thou art Peter [the Greek word Petros, literally a "little rock"], and upon this rock [Petra, a foundation rock, Christ the Rock, not Peter] I will build my church." Literally what Jesus told Peter is this: "You are a little rock, but on Myself, the great foundation Rock, I will build My church."

You should read the Catholic Fathers and you would see that this is the teaching that was once current among the best Catholic theologians. But when the church decided to pronounce the pope infallible, then the church decided to insist upon this dogma, that the church is founded on Peter, that that author-ity is now in the pope. But at that Council in 1870, you ought to know if you are an informed Catholic, that Bishop Strossmeyer then publicly said in a brilliant speech before the Cardinals what I am saying to you now, that the Bible clearly teaches that Christ Himself is the foundation of the church, not Peter. You are not allowed of course to read the Bible and to study and find what it means if that differs from the Catholic dogma. Once it was proper for the Bible to mean this. Now the Catholic hierarchy has determined it is to mean something else and so you of course as a good Catholic will go by tradition and dogma instead of by the Bible.

Peter himself was inspired to teach that Christ was the Rock on which the church and Christians are built.

"...The Lord is gracious. To whom coming, as unto a living stone, disal-

lowed indeed of men, but chosen of God, and precious, Ye also, as lively stones, are built up a spiritual house...."—I Pet. 2:3–5.

Converts come to Christ and thus as living stones are built on the Living Stone into a spiritual house. The same Scripture goes on to say that Jesus is not only the foundation stone, but the Head of the Corner, the Rock of Offense, the Stone of Stumbling. Throughout the Bible, again and again, Christ is called the Stone, the Rock. He is illustrated by the rock in the wilderness which Moses struck and from which came water for the thirsty multitude. In Daniel, chapter 2, He is pictured as the stone that will come at His Second Coming and smite the kings of the earth and destroy them.

No, the church is not founded on Peter. Incidently, there is no evidence whatever that Peter was ever in Rome. Paul wrote the book of Romans by divine inspiration and gave greeting to many, and Peter is not even mentioned. Twenty-nine people are called by name to whom Paul sends greetings, one whole church and a number of households. And Peter is not even mentioned. Why? He was not in Rome, of course.

In the book of Acts we are told how Paul came to Rome; we learn about those who came to greet him. We learn that he dwelt two whole years in his own hired house and that leading Jews came to meet him there. Peter did not come. Peter is not mentioned. Why? Peter was not in Rome. There is not a single reputable history in the world that even mentions Peter's being at Rome. The Bible does not mention it. In fact, when his epistles were written, Peter was in the other direction, at Babylon, and sends greetings from Babylon (I Peter 5:13). The idea of Peter's being at Rome is one of the fictions like all the "nails from the true cross," like literally thousands of fake "relics" honored by the fictions, the tradition, the superstitions of the church at Rome.

III. There Was No Pope, Neither Peter Nor Anybody Else, Among New Testament Christians.

You refer to Matthew 16:19 when Christ said to Peter, "And I will give unto thee the keys of the kingdom of heaven: and whatsoever thou shalt bind on earth shall be bound in heaven: and whatsoever thou shalt loose on earth shall be loosed in heaven."

1. The "keys" Jesus gave Peter did not mean he had power to forgive sins.

That does not mean what you think it means. A great theologian says on this verse:

"Not the keys of the church, but of the kingdom of heaven in the sense of Matthew 13., i.e. the sphere of Christian profession. A key is a badge of power or authority (cf. Isa. 22:22; Rev. 3:7). The apostolic history explains and limits this trust, for it was Peter who opened the door of Christian opportunity to Israel on the day of Pentecost (Acts 2:38–42), and to Gentiles in the house of Cornelius (Acts 10:34–46). There was no assumption by Peter of any other authority (Acts 15:7–17). In the council James, not Peter, seems to have presided (Acts 15:19; cf. Gal. 2:11–15). Peter claimed no more for himself than to be an apostle by gift (I Pet. 1:1), and an elder by office (I Pet. 5:1).

"The power of binding and loosing was shared (Matt. 18:18; John 20:23) by the other disciples. That it did not involve the determination of the eternal destiny of souls is clear from Revelation 1:18. The keys of death and the place of departed spirits are held by Christ alone" (notes in the *Scofield Reference Bible*).

> "Verily I say unto you, Whatsoever ye shall bind on earth shall be bound in heaven: and whatsoever ye shall loose on earth shall be loosed in heaven. Again I say unto you, That if two of you shall agree on earth as touching any thing that they shall ask, it shall be done for them of my Father which is in heaven."–Matt. 18:18, 19.

So not only to Peter, but to the other apostles and even to all Christians is the same promise given. Whatsoever they shall bind on earth shall be bound in Heaven; whatsoever they shall loose on earth shall be loosed in Heaven. And He says plainly, "That if two of you shall agree on earth as touching any thing that they shall ask, it shall be done for them of my Father which is in heaven." It is clear that Jesus is here talking about the power of prayer. The Christian who moves God can move everything that God moves. And if the Spirit of God leads Christians to unite in believing prayer, then they can have whatever they ask. This is exactly what was promised Peter; he could bind on earth things that would be bound in Heaven and loose on earth things that would be loosed in Heaven the same way that other Christians have exactly the same promise. Peter was simply a New Testament Christian. He had all the promises that God gave to the other apostles and all the promises God gave to other Christians. Even you surely would not say that the instruction in Matthew, chapter 18, was for the apostles only. And certainly you would not say it was for Peter only. So the promise about binding and loosing was to all the apostles, and more than that, it was for all Christians who, led by the Spirit of God, could agree to ask of God.

Now see John 20:21-23:

> "Then said Jesus to them again, Peace be unto you: as my Father hath sent me, even so send I you. And when he had said this, he breathed on them and saith unto them, Receive ye the Holy Ghost: Whose soever sins ye remit, they are remitted unto them; and whose soever sins ye retain, they are retained."–John 20:21-25.

Jesus is risen from the dead. He gives His disciples again the Great Commission and says, "As my Father hath sent me, even so send I you." And then He breathed on them and said, "Receive ye the Holy Ghost." And in connection with the Spirit of God on these Christians, He says, "Whose soever sins ye remit, they are remitted unto them; and whose soever sins ye retain, they are retained."

2. All apostles were equal with Peter.

Again, it is important to notice that this promise was not given to Peter alone, but to all the disciples present. Certainly the other apostles were there besides Thomas, and almost equally certain others were there besides the apostles. In the same chapter Mary Magdalene, Mary the mother of Jesus, and others are mentioned in connection with that group who saw Jesus after

His resurrection, and the women talked with the men about it. In Acts 1:13 and 14 we are told that the apostles "with the women, and Mary the mother of Jesus, and with his brethren," that is, the brothers of Jesus, who would include Jude, Simon, James, etc., were together.

So to this group of Christians in John 20 Jesus gave the promise: first, they were to have the Holy Spirit abiding in them. Then they were to go to fulfill the Great Commission.

Now note that Great Commission as it is stated again, in Matthew 28:19 and 20. That Great Commission was given to the apostles and other Christians there. But they were taught that when they got other disciples, they were to have them baptized and then to teach them, the new converts, "to observe all things whatsoever I have commanded you." Whatever command Jesus gave in the Great Commission is for every Christian, not only for the apostles and certainly not only for Peter. And that command is to be fulfilled in the power of the Holy Spirit, not in human wisdom.

Now notice verse 23, "Whose soever sins ye remit, they are remitted unto them; and whose soever sins ye retain, they are retained." Actually this verse is written in the Greek so it could be either present or pluperfect in time, that is, "Whose soever sins ye remit, they shall have been remitted unto them; and whose soever sins ye retain, they shall have been retained." So Dr. J. R. Mantey, professor of Greek, told me. In other words, led by the Holy Spirit a Christian who knows that one has trusted Christ for salvation can say, "Your sins have been remitted," knowing that they have already been remitted as soon as he trusted Christ. And to one who does not trust Christ, a Christian shall say, "Your sins are not remitted, they are retained, they are on you now," knowing that they have not been remitted, because the one did not trust Christ.

In the first place, it is certain that whatever the Lord said to Peter about any authority here, He said to the other apostles also. There was no primacy given Peter in this matter. And it is also equally clear that whatever authority any people had here, it was by the Spirit of God and in accordance with the Word of God, not that they could forgive sins, but they could know that the sins were forgiven one who trusted Christ or they could know that one's sins were not forgiven if he did not trust Christ.

To make it so any man could forgive sins on his own initiative would be utterly foreign to the clear teaching of the Bible elsewhere. That is human tradition which contradicts the plain Word of God and brings upon all who thus add to the Word the plagues and curses that Jesus warned of in Revelation 22:18 and 19.

Obviously, even the most casual reader of the Bible knows that New Testament Christians did not regard Peter as having any special authority. Paul found him wrong in the matter of a certain compromise, and so in Galatians, chapter 2, we find that Paul rebuked Peter openly to his face. Peter had no authority which Paul respected more than the authority of anyone else.

In the general council which met at Jerusalem in Acts, chapter 15, it seems that James presided and had the final word. Peter gave his word, as was proper, but he did not speak with any authority recognized by anybody present except the authority of good advice and the Holy Spirit's leading, such as James had also and as others had also on the same occasion.

No, there was no such thing as the Roman Catholic Church in Bible times. There was no popery. There was no mass and no sacrifices. There was no confessional, no pretense on the part of anyone that he could forgive sins. There was no priesthood except the priesthood of all believers in that we can pray for others. But there was no official priesthood in the churches. Roman Catholicism has changed elders and preachers into priests, has changed the pulpit into an altar, has changed Mary into "Mother of God, Queen of Heaven," etc., in idolatry.

3. The apostles had no successors; they handed down no authority.

Twelve original disciples of Jesus were called in the Bible "apostles." They were men specially sent and authorized to teach and preach until the Scriptures should be fulfilled. When Judas, by his sin, fell from the apostleship and killed himself, the disciples elected Matthias to be a witness with them of the resurrection of Christ, and the requirement was that he must be one who had been with them all the way from the baptism of Jesus by John the Baptist until His resurrection and could give witness of these things (Acts 1:22). Later Paul, Barnabas, and James, the brother of Jesus, are called apostles.

But in I Corinthians 12:28 we are told: "And God hath set some in the church, first apostles, secondar-ily prophets, thirdly teachers, after that miracles, then gifts of healings, helps, governments, diversities of tongues." The apostles were set first in the church. They had no successors. Peter did not give his apostolic authority to Mark who worked with him. Paul did not give his apostolic authority to Timothy, his beloved son in the ministry. John did not give his apostolic authority to anybody else. There is a wicked, foolish, unscriptural idea abroad that the "true church" is a matter of "apostolic succession." That idea was invented by the modern Roman Catholic Church. It was unknown in Bible times. And now when the Anglicans claim "apostolic succession in the priesthood," we know that they got it from Rome. They did not get it from the Bible. When our "Church of Christ" friends claim that they have the only true church, we know that that idea of a church was derived from Roman Catholic tradition. It is true that Christ said, "Upon this rock [and He meant Jesus] I will build my church; and the gates of hell shall not prevail against it" (Matt. 16:18). But He did not mean any organization on earth. The churches and congregations of Bible times have all disappeared. That "general assembly and church of the firstborn, which are written in heaven," the body of Christ, has not disappeared and will not disappear and the gates of Hell shall not prevail against it. But to claim that of any organization of men with human officers, is an idea foreign to the Bible and unsubstantiated by history.

The present so-called Roman Catholic Church is not the church at Rome to which Paul wrote his letter. It has none of the works. It does not believe the same doctrines. It does not have the simple local organization, local pastors (or bishops) and deacons. It does not preach the same plan of salvation. It does not have the same spiritual power.

Summing up, Peter had no authority that other apostles did not have, and that authority was never transmitted to anybody. Peter was not a pope, and even if he had been, he could not have handed that authority down to anybody else. All that is a web of human tradition and is of later origin manufactured by men and not after the Bible pattern. There is not a trace of the papacy in the Bible or in the New Testament church, either in organization or doctrine.

IV. The Authority Claimed by the Catholic Church Is Blasphemous and Unchristian.

The pope claims (in this modern dogma of the Catholic Church, which has developed particularly since the fourth Lateran Council in A. D. 1870, when papal infallibility was adopted as a dogma of the church) to be the vicegerent of God on earth, claims to speak with the authority of God, claims that when he and priests under him speak officially, it is God speaking. And you say, "His church represents Him (and you mean the Roman Catholic Church or hierarchy) just as He so stated 'as the Father hath sent me, even so send I you.'" But you certainly read the Scripture very carelessly. Individual Christians represent Christ. It was not to "the church," some super-duper world-wide organization, that Jesus said, "As my Father hath sent me, even so send I you"; it was to a group of individuals and He breathed on them and said, "Receive ye the Holy Ghost." And that day the Holy Spirit moved into the body of Christians to live and to represent Christ on earth.

The Holy Spirit Himself is Christ's own personal representative, His vicegerent on earth. And so the Bible carefully teaches. The Lord Jesus said nothing about breathing on the Roman Catholic Church the day He rose from the dead. There was no such church then. Such an idea among New Testament Christians was not even thought of.

And though there was a local group of Christians, He was not speaking to the group as an entity, but he was speaking to individuals. The Holy Spirit moves into the body of a Christian when he is saved. "What? know ye not that your body is the temple of the Holy Ghost which is in you, which ye have of God, and ye are not your own? For ye are bought with a price: therefore glorify God in your body, and in your spirit, which are God's" (I Cor. 6: 19, 20).

You say, "My Protestant friends do not seem to be able to see the necessity for having an organization, with a ruling authority in the greatest institution on earth." But you use the term "institution" in an unscriptural sense. The Bible does not even mention such an "institution." And you are trying to settle by human argument a matter which was brought on by human tradition, when if God had intended any such authority in an organization, that is, an organization which could save or damn, could forgive or not forgive, which could tell people whether they could read the Bible or not, whether they could follow the Bible or not–if God had wanted to put any such author-ity in an organization, He could have done so. He did not. The Bible never mentions anything of the kind.

You see, the trouble is you want a human author-ity, a man, to boss this matter when God wants the Holy Spirit to boss. You want that authority to reach down so a priest can tell people what they can do and what they cannot do, and God wants the Holy Spirit to dwell in the body of every believer and tell him what to do. And then you speak about "chaos" and say, "That is the situation in Protestantism today–'a house divided against itself.' " And you speak about "the Presbyterian branch." Again, you are using the term *church* in a wholly unscriptural sense not even thought of in the Bible. And Protestantism is not a church in the Bible sense any more than the Catholic organization is a church in the Bible sense.

V. Christians Who Set Out to Live by the Bible Have a Warm Bible Christianity and Spiritual Unity Utterly Unknown by Catholics.

You talk with no knowledge of the facts when you speak

about "chaos" among Bible believers. No, there is a chaos if you mean that there are many cults who, like Roman Catholics, set up some other standard to follow besides the Bible. Some groups who call themselves Protestant do not believe in the virgin birth, and others, like Catholics, say they believe in the virgin birth, but they do not believe in salvation by per-sonal faith in Christ. Of course, that is confusion whether among Catholics or Protestants, but it is not brought on by following the Bible, but rather by rejecting the Bible. Those who follow the Book of Mormon or Mrs. Mary Baker Eddy's writings, or who follow the "scientific" unbelief of religious liberals, or the traditions and rulings of the church among Catholics—these all, whether Protestants or Catholics, are in confusion, and of course do not represent Bible Christianity.

However, there is a remarkable unity, very easily demonstrated and known by millions of Christians, among Bible believers. It is a foolish saying of infidels that there "are some three hundred denominations and everybody understands the Bible differently." The simple truth is that all the principal groups of Christians in the world who bow to no authority but the Bible authority do agree on all the principal doctrines in the Bible. Christians from a hundred different denominations, I suppose, from year to year attend Moody Bible Institute, or the Bible Institute of Los Angeles, or other fundamental Bible institutes where the authority of the Word of God is held up always above any other source of doc-trine, above any authority of denomination or pope or bishop or council or cardinals or priests.

I am editor of an interdenominational Christian magazine. We have, among those who read The SWORD OF THE LORD reg-ularly, almost every kind of divergent denomination from priests in the Filipino Catholic Church to those from all principal Protestant bodies. I received the other day a most fervent, broth-erly letter from a Lutheran minister. He sprinkles babies; he has a liturgy and there are other minor matters on which we would differ. But on the great issues of the verbally inspired Bible, the deity of Christ, His virgin birth, His blood atonement, His bodily resurrection, on the need for a new birth, on Heaven and Hell, we feel as brothers.

I have held great city-wide campaigns in Chicago, Buffalo, Cleveland, Seattle, Miami, and elsewhere, with representatives of the principal Protestant groups taking part in those meetings, with the simple stipulation that they must be men who believed the Bible and the essentials of the Christian faith. And so Baptists, Presbyterians, Nazarenes, Pentecostalists, Mennonites, Episcopalians, and many others have participated in those meetings. The one simple essential we agreed on was that the Bible was the Word of God and was the supreme authority and the Christ of the Bible is all He claimed to be. So such people naturally agreed on the great doctrines of the Bible, the verbal inspiration, the deity of Christ, His virgin birth, His blood atonement, His bodily resurrection, His miracles, and the need for regeneration, salvation by faith in Christ, Heaven and Hell, etc. It is a foolish and insincere fiction to suppose that there is a chaos among Bible-believing Christians. That simply is not so.

You understand, of course, there were many, many who could not properly take part in such a campaign with me as a preacher and they would not have been welcome. That would include all those false cults who have some other authority besides the Bible. Mormons would not fit in, nor Christian Scientists, nor Catholics, nor Jehovah's Witnesses, because all of these have sources other than the fundamental center of a Christian unity, the Bible. They would not agree in doctrine because they get their doctrines out of human tradition or the writings of Mrs. Mary Baker Eddy, or the Book of Mormon, or the books of Judge Rutherford, instead of from the Bible. I am saying simply that the Holy Spirit living in the bodies of Christians who believe the Bible and go to the Bible for authority have more unity than would be possible in a great organization such as the Catholic Church where the authority is supposed to reside in the church (meaning literally in the priesthood and not in the congregations).

I preached the Gospel in the First Presbyterian Church in Inchon, Korea, where General McArthur made his famous landing in the Korean War. In that foreign country, speaking through an interpreter, standing barefooted upon a pillow, preaching to people who sat cross-legged on a polished floor, I found exactly the same sweet unity of spirit, the same brotherly love that I found with Christians in Bombay and Madras, India, in Karuizawa, Japan, and as I found in great united meetings all over America.

The other day a Catholic man who had lost his wife and was disconsolate and now for three years had been trying to raise his children alone, found that he too had this same unity with other Bible-believing Christians. He went regularly to the Catholic Church and to no other, but he said, "It was like a trip to the corner store, with no spiritual help." His hungry heart reached out for something and he began to read the Bible at home to his children. He began to listen to my broadcast. His heart began to seek for a personal acquaintance with Jesus Christ. He wrote to me pleading for prayers and help. Some godly people went to see him; they read together from the Bible and he was taught to look to Jesus who died to save sinners. On his knees he trusted Christ and took Him as Saviour and, oh, how happy he has been since! Mark you, this happiness, this union of heart with other Christians, did not come through the Catholic organization. It came as he read the Bible, and then found other Christians who believed the Bible and then found the Christ of the Bible.

The "chaos" that you pretend to see among Bible believers is simply not true. There is a chaos among those who have other sources of doctrine and so serve other gods. There is a chaos when men go to Catholic tradition or the Book of Mormon or the writings of Mrs. Mary Baker Eddy or the presumptuous imaginings of modernists or unbelievers. But there is a great unity which millions know as they read the Bible and find there the same Saviour, the same doctrine that all have sinned, the same promise that the blood of Christ has paid for our sins and that Christ died for us and is willing to forgive sinners, and then the sweet sense of fellowship of born-again believers who know they have a home in Heaven and who know they are born of God.

VI. Roman Catholics Themselves Do Not Have This Christian Unity.

There is a kind of unity among the loyal adherents of the Catholic Church, but it is not Christian unity. It is not even the kind of unity that men have in a labor union where they join voluntarily, where they have a vote in the proceedings, where they can argue for their rights, and where they can join others of like convictions to seek a common end.

Catholics do not have the unity which comes when people know the same Saviour, have the same peace in heart, find in the Bible the same doctrines and look together, as the Bible teaches us to do, for Christ's Second Coming. Catholics are alike in praying to Mary, but Mary does not answer, does not give them any spiritual response. The unity of Catholics is like the unity in a penitentiary. The prisoners have someone to tell them what to do. They are told when to get up, when to march to the playground, when to go to meals, and when to rise. They are fed not what they want, but what prison officials decide is proper on the budget that is provided. Prisoners have something in common: they have the same kind of bars on their cells, the same concrete floor, the same smell of disinfectant.

I am saying the Catholics do not know the kind of unity which is very common among Bible-believing Christians. Have a bunch of Catholics together; now try to have a testimony meeting and try to get them to rise with joy in their faces and tell how God has answered their prayers. A few Catholics, thank God, have had such experiences. They seem queer to other Catholics and that is not the ordinary thing.

Other Christians find a common bond in the Bible. But sadly I have found that the average Catholic family does not even have a Catholic Bible. If they have one, they are not free to study it and find what God Himself means to tell them. They are to believe the Bible teaches only what the church tells them it teaches. The simple truth is that the Catholic Church through the centuries has usually forbidden Catholics to study the Bible and now in our American civilization public enlightenment has made it so they must give permission for Catholics to read the Bible. Catholics generally are not encouraged to read it and generally do not read it.

I remember I talked to a beautiful and cultured Catholic lady in Washington, D. C. A question came up about the Bible and I said I would ask her a question. She threw up her hands and laughed deprecatingly and said, "Oh no! I don't know a thing about the Bible. Now on the Prayer Book," she said, "I am pretty good. But I don't know anything about the Bible." I say that that attitude is rather characteristic of good Catholics. Those who are not good Catholics are not usually good on the Prayer Book, even. Catholics are not usually tied together by one common experience of conversion. They are not commonly tied together with a sweet enjoyment of the same Scripture truths. Catholics generally believe in the virgin birth, and I thank God that they do, but that is emphasized primarily in order to emphasize Mary, and not necessarily to emphasize the deity of Christ.

And in most of the Catholic countries in the world, as in South American countries, priests systematically collect and burn Bibles and people are taught that it is heresy to read the Bible. And that attitude is the general Catholic attitude around the world except in a very few enlightened spots where culture makes for more human freedom than will permit that degree of servility.

You talk of Catholic unity. The simple truth is that most of the Catholic population of the world lives in most abject superstition and ignorance, with almost no comprehension of spiritual truths. In countries like Columbia and Peru in South America, Protestant missionaries have recently been murdered, arid nationals who have been converted to Christ and come to know Him as Saviour and do riot depend on the priest for forgiveness have their homes burned, and many a believer has been beaten and others tortured and killed. There is no more unity among Catholics than the kind of unity of communist-inspired mobs in Castro's Cuba.

Do not misunderstand me. I do not mean that Catholics are communists, or that the Catholic Church generally favors communism. I mean that the priest-led mobs who killed Christians who read the Bible in South America are the victims of mass superstitions and mob rages such as similar mobs in Cuba are, who storm the homes of Americans.

You speak of unity among Catholics. But President Kennedy does not agree with the Catholic dogma that every head of state, if a Catholic, must be subject to the pope in his official duties. On this matter Catholics in America do not very well agree with Catholics in Italy.

The true and loyal Catholic knows nothing of the great freedom in Christ. He does not know that he can come personally to Christ and get forgiveness without any reference to the priest or the church or the mass or the confessional. He does not know the great freedom taught in that Scripture, I Timothy 2:5 and 6: "For there is one God, and one meditator between God and men, the man Christ Jesus; Who gave himself a ransom for all, to be testified in due time." He does not know. that he can go to Christ directly and that Christ has made peace between him and God. No, the Catholic Church has put Mary in there as an intermediary and the saints and the priests and the church.

I can read the Bible and ask God's blessed Spirit to help me understand it. That is exactly what Jesus taught His disciples, that "when he, the Spirit of truth, is come, he will guide you into all truth" (John 16:13). But that blessed and intimate fellowship with the Holy Spirit leading him to understand God's Word, the Catholic is not free to have. He cannot go to the Bible and find whether it is proper to eat meat on Friday or during Lent—no, he must go to the church who has established the man-made rules.

So the Catholic has little acquaintance with Christ, little dependence on the Holy Spirit. It is a big church, a big priesthood, a little Jesus. It is a big Mary but a little Saviour. It is big law but little grace.

VII. No True Roman Catholic Is Sure of Heaven.

A noble young Catholic man wrote me. He was greatly impressed with The SWORD OF THE LORD. He appealed to me that I would enter "the true church." How much good I would do, he said, if I would join the Roman Catholic Church and use whatever gifts and training I have in advancing the cause of "the true church."

I wrote him that I could not do that, first of all, because as it is now I have perfect assurance that my sins are forgiven; I have the assurance from the Word of God and from the Holy Spirit who lives within me that when I took Christ as my Saviour and relied upon Him, my sins were all forgiven and there, once for all, as they were paid for on the cross, my sins were forgiven, I was born of God and I am certain of Heaven. I told him I do not deserve this salvation, that it is all of God's grace, but it is certain because the blood of Jesus paid for it; I do not have to go through the church to get this salvation; I have already gone to Christ and when I trusted Him I received everlasting life. I told him that I could not give up this sweet peace and assurance.

I told him that I am relying on the one sacrifice for-ever which perfected the one who trusted in Christ according to Hebrews 10:10–14, and that now I could not put any confidence in the mass, since, after my sins were remitted through the blood of Christ, "there is no more offering for sin" (Heb. 10:18). And I urged him to find out if his priest, or if any other Catholic he knew, had sweet peace and assurance that his sins are already all forgiven, that he is now already a child of God and certain for Heaven, with all his sins forever hidden under the blood of Christ.

He was indignant. He was sure Catholics had just as much

peace and assurance as anyone else did. So he went to his local priest in Tennessee. That priest assured him that no, of course, he did not know for sure that his sins were all forgiven. He hoped to go to Heaven but he would probably have to go to purgatory for a time first.

The young man was distressed so he went to a bishop and there he received the same kind of an answer. Now, getting desperate, he wrote to a number of archbishops. And again he got the same kind of answer, that none of them could know for sure that their sins were forgiven.

Distressed he went back to the local priest and asked the priest why now there would be the sacrifice of the mass when the Bible so plainly said that Jesus had paid the whole debt by one offering forever, and that "now...there is no more offering for sin."

The priest scoffed at him. "Who gave you the right to interpret the Bible?" he stormed at the young man.

The young man, cut to the quick, said to the priest, "Who gave you the right to say that there is need for more offerings when the Bible says that Jesus' offering settled the matter once for all?" The priest, instead of answering him, angrily slapped his face and turned and left him.

That young man went to bed that night but tossed in torment for hours. Could no one then have any assurance of forgiveness? Was there no certainty of salvation through the blood of Christ, to one who trusted in Him? And in his groping mind there came again the Scripture of Hebrews 10:10: "By the which will we are sanctified through the offering of the body of Jesus Christ once for all," and there he put his trust in the Lord Jesus alone and had the peace that he could not have by Catholic dogma.

I have from time to time, contact with Catholics whom I greatly love and respect. Many of them are noble, good people and some of them, I believe, are devout Christians, by which I mean that in spite of all the false teachings of the traditions of the church, they have seen through the darkness and have come to personally trust in Jesus Christ and His atoning blood, and have rested in that and have peace as born-again children of God. But I would have to say in honesty that that is not the position of the average Catholic. And that peace, that assurance of salvation, that personal devotion to Jesus Christ, is not known by the average Catholics. They know Mary and penances and Ave Marias and confessionals, but the sweet joy of settled peace, knowing sins are forgiven, knowing they are children of God, knowing they are born again, knowing they are saved and going to Heaven (and mark you, all these are Bible principles)–I say that is unusual among Catholics and that kind of settled peace of certain salvation is not usually the property of Catholics.

No, dear brother, when you talk to me about the unity of the Catholic Church, you are not talking about any Christian unity such as real born-again Christians generally have when they depend on the Word of God alone as authority and when they come to Christ personally for salvation and when they have the Holy Spirit dwelling within to guide them into the truth and comfort them.

VIII. The Autocratic Domineering of the Catholic Church Over Its Members Dishonors Christ and the Bible.

I have indicated above that the Catholic does not have the peace and happiness and freedom and spiritual enlightenment that one has who is free to go to the Bible and take the authority of the Bible and the leadership of God's own Spirit dwelling within his body. But not only the Catholic who is domineered and ruled and bossed suffers. The Catholic must eat fish (or macaroni and cheese) on Fridays and during Lent. If he reads the Bible at all he cannot find out what it means except from a Catholic theologian or some of the official literature of the church. He dare not depend on the Spirit of God to make plain the Word of God.

And not only does the poor Catholic suffer, but Christ Himself suffers too. His crown rights are vio-lated! The Lord Jesus who seeks to be Lord of all is put second to Mary, second to the saints and second to the rigmarole. And the blood of Christ is not the one great element that settles salvation for the believing sinner; the great element is the church itself which may choose to dole out bit by bit any blessings that may be obtained through the blood. The Catholic's sins are forgiven only if the priest says so (and he never knows for sure then). The Catholic need not pray as to where he should help support the Gospel to get it out to all the world. The church decides that for him. And so Christ has to step into the background. Every time you have a high church you have a low Jesus. Every time you have a high human priesthood you have a low divine Saviourhood. There are too many lords in the Catholic Church for Christ Jesus to be Lord of all as He claims to be and wants to be.

Do not misunderstand me, Catholics are not alone in this matter. Many Protestants and other false cults take away the liberty that is in Christ. Christ as so-called "Way Shower," must share honors with Mrs. Mary Baker Eddy, "The Leader." Or some others teach that one cannot be saved without baptism and so Jesus has to step back a bit into the background so that baptism and the church and the preacher may take a more important place. And when Southern Baptists insist that one does not truly serve God except as he supports the Co-operative Program or the denomination, that is the same kind of popery that dishonors Christ and puts the church, the organization, the leadership, the secretariat ahead of Christ and the Holy Spirit. And the pastor who insists that the tithes will not be recognized by God unless the tithes come into the church where this pastor receives his salary and where he can dominate the spending of the money—that pastor takes the part of the same popery that puts Christ in second place and puts human instruments or traditions or commandments ahead of the authority of the Holy Spirit and the authority of Christ.

But that great state church pictured in Revelation 17 with

headquarters in the city of the seven hills (Rev. 17:9), that harlot woman that is called "the mother of harlots and abominations in the earth," that state church "drunken with the blood of the saints and with the blood of the martyrs of Jesus"–she is the mother of abominations and particularly the mother of this abomination of putting the church ahead of Christ, putting the ordinances ahead of Christ, putting human leaders ahead of Christ and putting the tradition and commandments of men ahead of the Word of God.

I am saying that the overlordship of the Catholic Church is not only unscriptural, utterly unknown in the Bible and in New Testament churches, but it dishonors Christ, it perverts Christianity, it takes from the Lordship of Christ, it denies the freedom of the human soul before God, and in that organization men take the leadership which God plainly gave to the Holy Spirit in the individual believer.

Dear Catholic Friend; I have written in love. After repeated correspondence and many, many questions and many arguments, I have felt led to go into detail. I have no hate for Catholics. I know many Catholics personally and love them. But I must protest that there is nothing like the Roman Catholic Church in the Bible. There is no papacy. There is no mass. There is no confessional. There are no prayers to Mary or to the saints. And nothing could please me better than that you, dear Catholic friend, could come out into the joy and peace and personal relationship with Christ which I enjoy, knowing that my sins are forgiven, knowing that by God's mercy I am ready for Heaven where He will take me when He comes or when I die.

In Jesus' name, yours,

John R. Rice

DEAR CATHOLIC FRIEND

The blood of Christ is the one great element that settles salvation for the believing sinner. Any other teaching is an assault on God's Word. It pushes Christ into the background, and His crown rights are violated!

The overlordship of any church or self-appointed spiritual leader is not only unscriptural; it dishonors Christ. Every time there is a high church, there is a low Jesus. Every time there is a human priesthood, there is a low divine Saviourhood.

Dear Catholic Friend is a detailed letter written in love by Dr. John R. Rice to an earnest Catholic man who repeatedly argued in favor of the Catholic Church.

"According to the grace of God which is given unto me, as a wise masterbuilder, I have laid the foundation, and another buildeth thereon. But let every man take heed how he buildeth thereupon.

"For other foundation can no man lay than that is laid, which is Jesus Christ."—I Cor. 3:10,11

224 Bridge Avenue • Murfreesboro, TN 37129
swordofthelord.com

ISBN 978-0-87398-152-1